THE UNIVERSE

THE OUTER PLANETS

NEIL ARDLEY

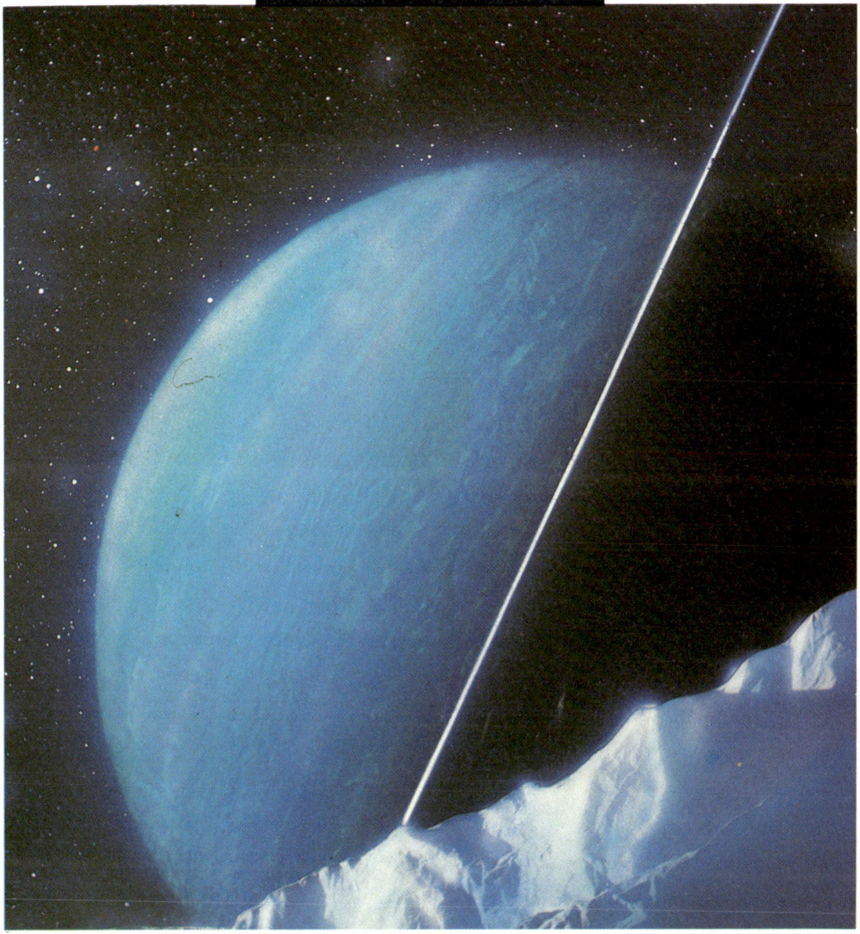

Editorial planning
Philip Steele

First published by Macmillan Education Ltd 1987
Reprinted with corrections 1991
by Heinemann Children's Reference,
a division of Heinemann Educational Books Ltd, Halley Court, Jordan Hill, Oxford OX2 8EJ
Companies and representatives throughout the world

Designed and produced by BLA Publishing Ltd,
East Grinstead, Sussex, England.

Illustrations by Sebastian Quigley/Linden Artists, Sallie Alane Reason, Steve Weston/Linden Artists
Colour origination by Waterden Reproductions Ltd
Printed in Hong Kong

British Library Cataloguing in Publication Data

Ardley, Neil
    The universe : outer planets.
    I. Planets – Juvenile literature
    I. Title
    523.4   QB602

ISBN 0–431–00766–7
ISBN 0–431–00763–2 Series

Photographic credits

t = top b = bottom l = left r = right

cover: Science Photo Library

5 Science Photo Library; 6 ZEFA; 7 Ann Ronan Picture Library; 9t, 9b Science Photo Library; 11 NASA/John Mason; 15, 16, 17t, 17b, 18, 19, 20/21 Science Photo Library; 22 Ann Ronan Picture Library; 23, 24/25, 26, 27, 28, 29, 32, 33, 35 Science Photo Library; 36, 37 NASA/John Mason; 41, 42, 43, 45 Science Photo Library

Note to the reader
In this book there are some words in the text which are printed in **bold** type. This shows that the word is listed in the glossary on page 46. The glossary gives a brief explanation of words which may be new to you.

Contents

Introduction

We live on a world called the **Earth**. It is a big ball of rock moving through space. Much of the Earth is covered with water and there is a thin layer of air around it. The Earth is almost 13 000 km across. If you could put the Earth on scales, it would weigh about 6 000 million million million tonnes!

The **Moon** is a smaller ball of rock which moves around the Earth. There are more worlds much farther away than the Moon. Some of them are much bigger than the Earth. All of the worlds are very different from ours. Some have giant **rings** around them. These worlds are so far away that they appear as dots of light in the night sky.

Paths through space

The Earth and the other big worlds are called **planets**. All the planets move through space. The paths they follow are called **orbits**. The planets travel around the **Sun**. The Sun is a great ball of glowing **gas** which lights up the planets. Many of the planets are circled by moons like our own. There are nine planets moving around the Sun. Together, the Sun and the planets make up the **Solar System**.

The Solar System is about 4600 million years old. It was formed from a cloud of **dust** and gas which was spinning in space. The Sun and its planets pull at each other with a force called **gravity**. Gravity keeps all the worlds moving in their orbits. It holds the Solar System together.

▼ The word 'solar' means 'to do with the Sun'. The Solar System is that part of space which comes under the pull of the Sun's gravity. All the planets orbit the Sun. The orbits of the giant outer planets lie beyond Mars.

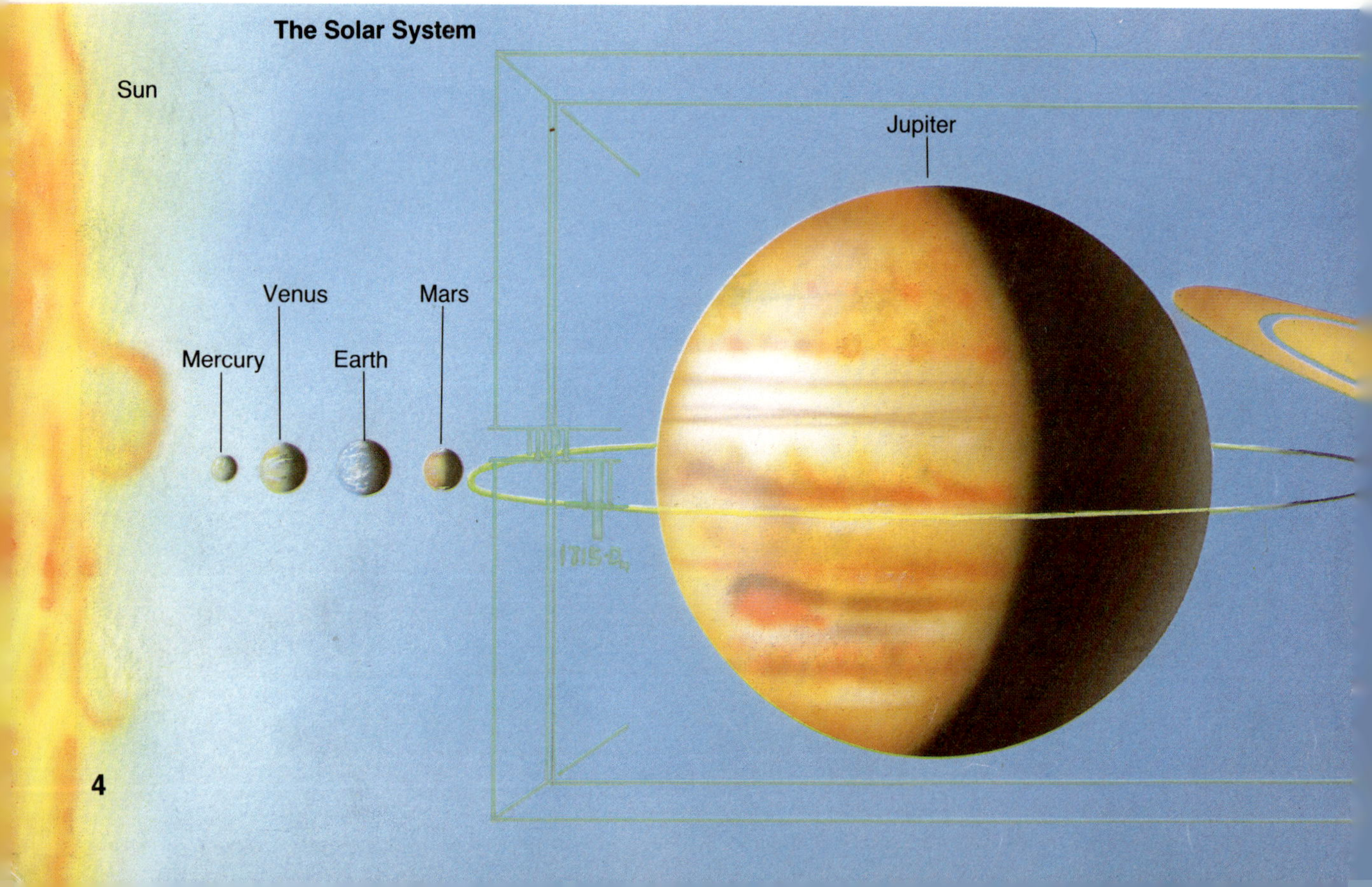

The Solar System

Sun

Jupiter

Venus

Mars

Mercury

Earth

Far from the Sun

The Sun is the nearest **star**. The heat and light of the Sun makes our planet Earth warm and bright. The Earth is one of four small, rocky planets that are nearest to the Sun. Mercury and Venus are closer to the Sun than we are. Mars is farther away.

Beyond Mars are five more planets. Four of them are giant worlds called Jupiter, Saturn, Uranus and Neptune. At the edge of the Solar System is tiny Pluto. When farthest away Pluto is over 7375 million km from the Sun. That is nearly 50 times farther away from the Sun than the Earth.

The Solar System is very big, but it is only a small part of the **Universe**. The Universe is everything that exists. It includes all the stars and the space between them. There are billions of stars in the Universe.

This book is about the five outer planets of the Sun's family. They move through distant parts of the Solar System. There it is bitterly cold and the Sun's light is dim. Jupiter and Saturn look like bright stars in the night sky. Uranus, Neptune and Pluto are much fainter. You need a **telescope** to see them.

▼ These colourful swirling clouds cover the giant planet Jupiter. They are at the top of a very deep layer of gases. Jupiter has no solid surface on which a spacecraft could land. People could not live there.

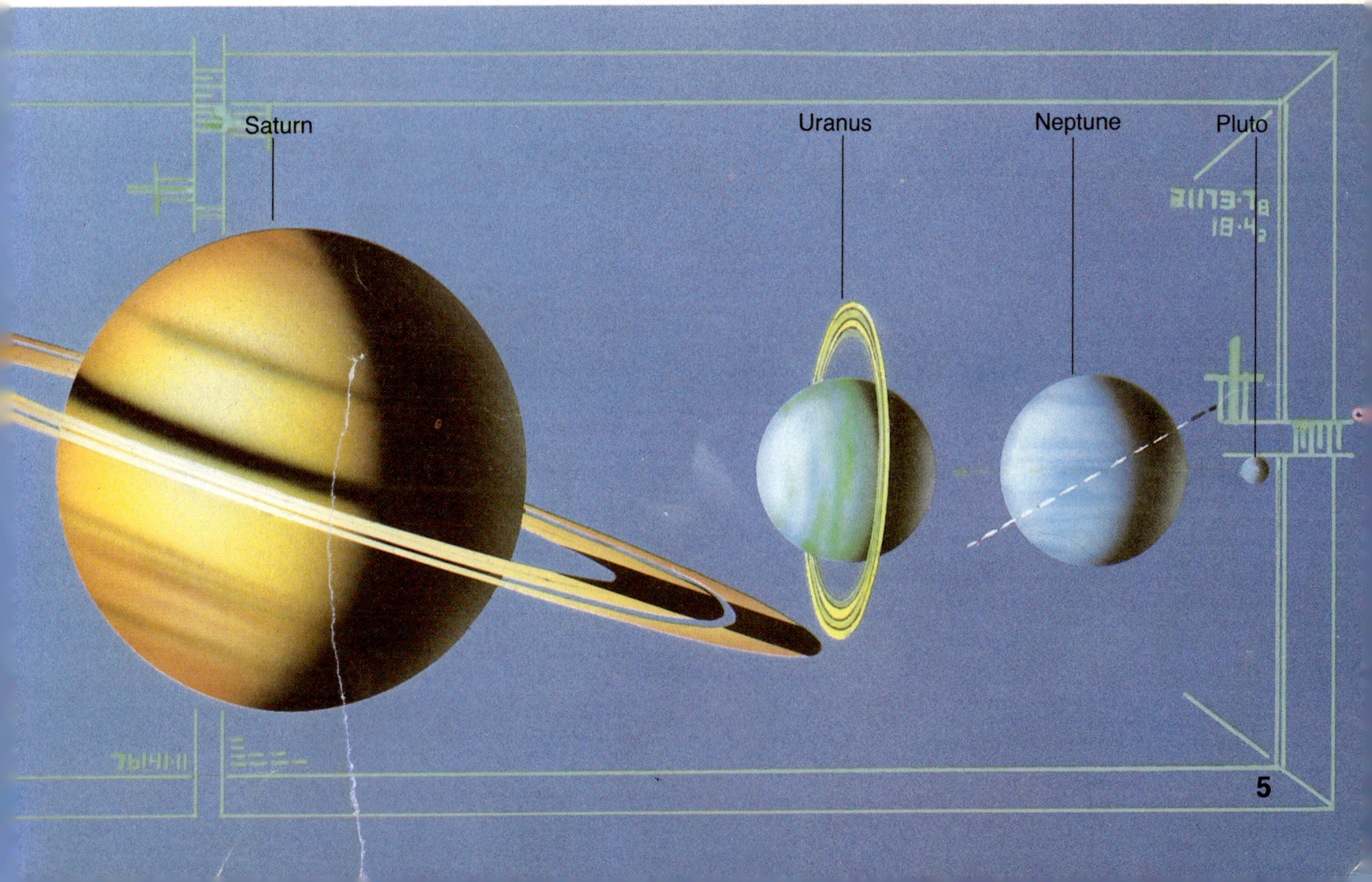

Saturn   Uranus   Neptune   Pluto

Planets in history

▼ The ruins of the temple of Saturn can still be seen in Rome. In ancient Rome, the story was told that Jupiter chased Saturn from the sky, and that he hid himself in Rome. The planet was named after the Roman god.

People who lived long ago knew about the planets. When they looked up into the night sky, they saw that five stars seemed to wander slowly through the sky. All the other stars stayed in the same places in the sky. The wandering 'stars' are in fact not stars at all. They are planets.

People used to think that gods and goddesses lived in the sky. Some people used to worship the Sun and Moon. Some people gave the names of gods and goddesses to the planets. The Romans could see two of the outer planets. They called them Jupiter and Saturn. These were the names of Roman gods.

Jupiter was the king of the gods. Jupiter happened to be a good name for the planet, which is the biggest in the Solar System. The Romans did not know this. Saturn was the father of Jupiter.

New worlds

For thousands of years, people thought there were only six planets. These were Earth and the five wandering 'stars' that they could see. For many years, people believed that the planets ruled their lives in some way. People thought that Saturn made them gloomy. Some people still believe such ideas today. They are called **astrologers**. Scientists who study planets and stars are called **astronomers**. They do not believe these ideas.

In 1608, a Dutchman called Hans Lippershey built the first telescope. When astronomers looked at the planets through telescopes, they could see that the planets are round worlds like the Earth. They could see that there were moons around Jupiter and rings around Saturn.

In 1781, an astronomer called William Herschel, who lived in England, found a new planet with a telescope he had made. The new planet was named Uranus after the Greek god of the Heavens. Other people thought that there might be other planets beyond Uranus. In 1846, a German called Johann Galle spotted Neptune. This planet was named after the Roman god of the sea. Pluto was discovered in 1930. Pluto was the Roman name for the god of the underworld. This was where the Romans thought people went after they died. With the discovery of Pluto, the ninth planet in the Solar System had been found.

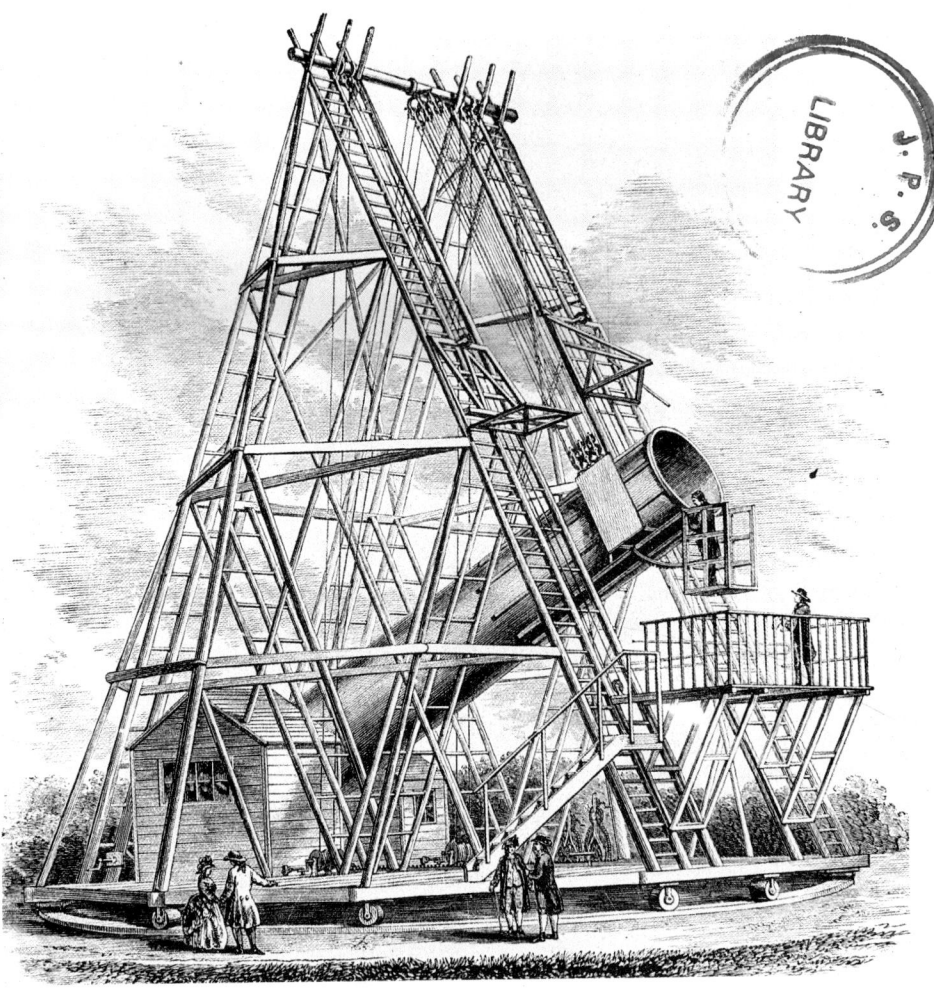

▶ **William Herschel was one of the greatest astronomers of all time. Although born in Germany, he moved to Bath in England. He built his own telescopes. On 13 March 1781 he saw a strange point of light in the sky through a small telescope he had made. He had found a new planet, now called Uranus. Herschel made the very large telescope shown here while living in Slough, near London. He used it to study the stars.**

The space age

We have very good photographs of most of the planets and their moons. They have been taken by cameras on board **space probes**. These are machines which are sent through space to the planets. They do not carry any people. The probes take close-up pictures of the planets. They use **radio signals** to send these pictures back to the Earth.

▼ The flight path of Voyager 2 has taken it past Jupiter, Saturn, Uranus and Neptune on its way out of the Solar System. It took thousands of photographs of these outer planets.

Out into space

A **rocket** launches a space probe into space at high speed. As the probe moves through space, it is controlled by a **computer** inside it. Radio signals may also be sent from Earth to the probe in order to tell the probe what to do.

The space probes that have flown to the outer planets did not land. Instead, they flew past the planets. They took photographs and also took measurements. The probes found out how cold the planets are. They studied the layer of gases around each planet. This layer is called the **atmosphere**.

The first space probe to visit the giant outer planets was Pioneer 10. It passed Jupiter in 1973. Pioneer 11 followed a year later. It also passed Saturn in 1979. Voyagers 1 and 2 visited Jupiter and Saturn. Voyager 2 went on to Uranus and Neptune.

Venus
Mercury
Earth
Sun
Mars
Jupiter
Saturn
Uranus
Neptune
Voyager 2

The future

The two Pioneer and two Voyager space probes are still moving through space. Eventually they will leave the Solar System. They will enter the space between our Sun and the other stars.

Space probes have now visited all of the planets except tiny Pluto. At the moment, there are no plans to send a probe to Pluto.

The Pioneer and Voyager probes flew past Jupiter and Saturn. They spent very little time close to the planets. In December 1995, a space probe called Galileo will arrive at Jupiter. It will spend two years studying Jupiter and its moons. Another space probe, called Cassini, is due to reach Saturn in 2002. Cassini will spend up to four years studying Saturn and its magnificent rings.

Perhaps people will visit the outer planets in the next century. The giant planets have no solid surfaces on which spacecraft could land. Instead, people may land on the moons of these planets.

▲ Pioneer 10 being prepared for its journey to the outer planets. It was launched by the United States. In 1973, Pioneer 10 became the first space probe to reach Jupiter.

▼ A painting showing Voyager 1 flying past Saturn and its rings. Eventually we shall lose touch with the two Voyager probes as they leave the Solar System.

Jupiter: the giant

Jupiter is the biggest of all the planets. The distance across a planet from one side to the other is called its **diameter**. Jupiter's diameter is 11 times that of the Earth. The amount of material in the planet, or its **mass**, is 318 times that of the Earth.

We see Jupiter easily because it is nearer to Earth and bigger than the other giant planets. It is usually the fourth brightest object in the sky after the Sun, Moon and Venus. Through a small telescope you will see Jupiter as a yellowish disc with markings on it.

Facts and figures

Jupiter is more than five times farther away from the Sun than Earth. This means that it takes much longer to go around the Sun once. Earth takes just one year. Jupiter takes nearly 12 years. The time a planet takes to go around the Sun is called its **period of revolution**.

As planets go around the Sun, they spin.

Jupiter spins more quickly than any other planet. The time a planet takes to spin around once is called its **period of rotation**. The Earth takes 24 hours. Jupiter spins once in less than 10 hours. This speed makes the planet bulge around its middle, or **equator**. The planet looks as if it is slightly squashed.

Planets spin around an **axis**. This is a line that we imagine to exist between a planet's most northern and southern points, or **poles**. The axis of Jupiter is tilted slightly towards the Sun.

Jupiter is so big that the pull of its gravity is very strong. If you could stand on Jupiter, you would weigh nearly three times as much as you do on Earth! The atmosphere contains gases that you could not breathe. Jupiter is not a planet where people could live.

▶ From Earth, Jupiter shines with a yellow light. If you look at the planet through a telescope you can see light and dark bands. These markings are shown in this picture sent back by the Voyager 1 space probe.

Facts about Jupiter	
Diameter	142 800 km
Mass	318 times that of Earth
Distance from the Sun	778 million km
Period of rotation	9 hours, 50 minutes
Period of revolution	11.9 years
Tilt of axis	3°
Gravity on the surface	2.7 times that of Earth
Temperature of cloud tops	−150°C
Atmosphere	hydrogen, helium
Number of moons	16

Earth   Jupiter

Jupiter: inside the planet

▼ Jupiter is a giant planet, but it is not solid. Inside, it is made mostly of liquid hydrogen in various forms. At the centre lies a small, rocky core. This planet gives out its own heat.

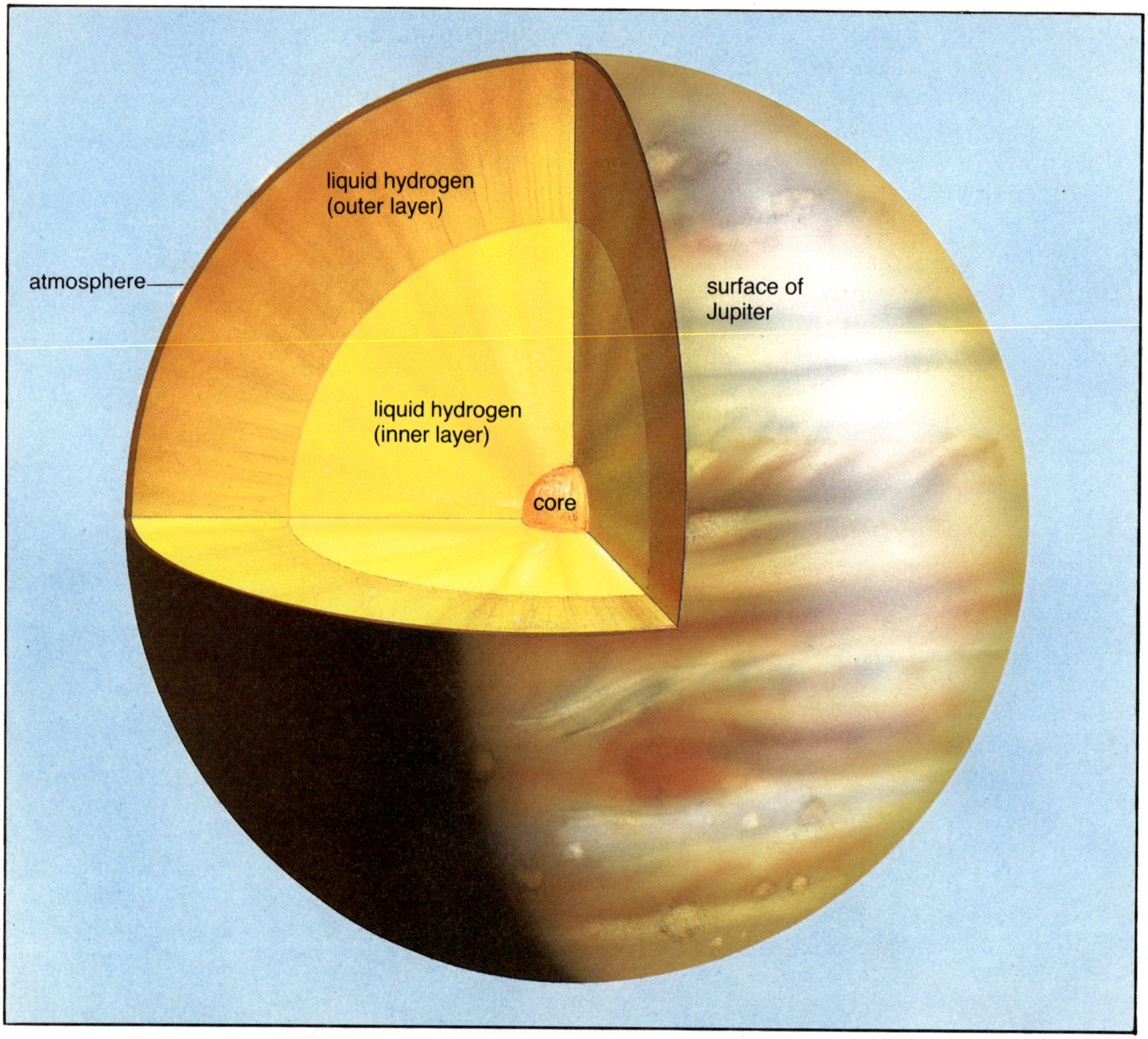

liquid hydrogen
(outer layer)

atmosphere

liquid hydrogen
(inner layer)

surface of
Jupiter

core

Jupiter is not like the Earth. Photographs from space probes show that huge bands of cloud circle the planet. Beneath the clouds, there is not a world like ours with mountains, valleys, rivers and deserts. In fact, there is no land at all. Jupiter is not a solid world. It is made up mostly of gases and liquids.

Most of Jupiter's atmosphere is made up of the gas called **hydrogen**. About a tenth of it is another gas called **helium**. The planet's atmosphere presses down on the layers below with such force that the hydrogen gas turns into a liquid. The inside of Jupiter is made up mostly of liquid hydrogen in various forms.

Inside Jupiter

Let us take a journey down to the centre of Jupiter. At the top of the atmosphere it is very cold, about −150°C. As we go down, the gases get thicker and warmer. After going down for 1000 km, the **pressure** is about 6000 times greater than the pressure of air upon the Earth. The temperature is 2000°C. Here the hydrogen gas turns into a liquid. 25 000 km below the cloud tops, the temperature reaches 11 000°C. The pressure is now three million times greater than on the Earth. Here the liquid hydrogen changes into a peculiar liquid that behaves like a metal. At the centre of the planet is a small **core** of rock. This is 10 to 20 times as heavy as the Earth.

Jupiter does not get much heat from the Sun because it is so far away. The planet makes its own heat deep inside. This heat rises up through the atmosphere and spreads evenly over the whole planet. The poles on Jupiter are no colder than the equator.

Forces in space

Strong **electric currents** may pass through the peculiar layer of liquid metallic hydrogen deep inside Jupiter. These surges of energy have an effect like that of a **magnet**. Magnets have the power to pull objects towards them or push them away. The region of force around a magnet is called a **magnetic field**. The electric currents inside Jupiter set up a magnetic field in the space around the planet.

This field traps **particles** or tiny specks of matter, which stream through space. The trapped particles form belts of deadly radiation around Jupiter. If people were to travel too close to these belts, they would be bombarded by particles and killed.

▼ Heat rises from the centre of Jupiter to the surface and passes into the atmosphere. It moves into belts of cooler gases which surround the planet.

hot gas rises

belt of cool gas

Jupiter: the storm clouds

Jupiter is the most colourful planet in the Solar System. The light and dark bands which surround the planet contain brightly coloured clouds. They are red, yellow, orange, white and blue. Some of the bands contain swirling and zigzag patterns.

Winds and lightning

The pattern of light and dark bands that we see is caused by winds that blow around Jupiter. The strongest winds near the equator blow from the west. They howl around the planet at speeds of up to 550 km an hour. To the north and south, the winds blow in bands, first from the east, then from the west. Near the poles, the wind patterns disappear. The winds carry clouds around the planet.

Huge bolts of lightning flash through the clouds. Rays from the Sun strike the gases too. These cause other gases to form. One gas is **ammonia**. Another gas is **hydrogen sulphide**. These gases have nasty smells. The gases mix together to form clouds of frozen **crystals** and drops of liquid. Clouds of different colours float at different heights in the atmosphere. At the top where it is coldest, there are red and white clouds. Then come yellow, orange and brown clouds. Beneath these are bluish clouds made of ice crystals or tiny drops of water.

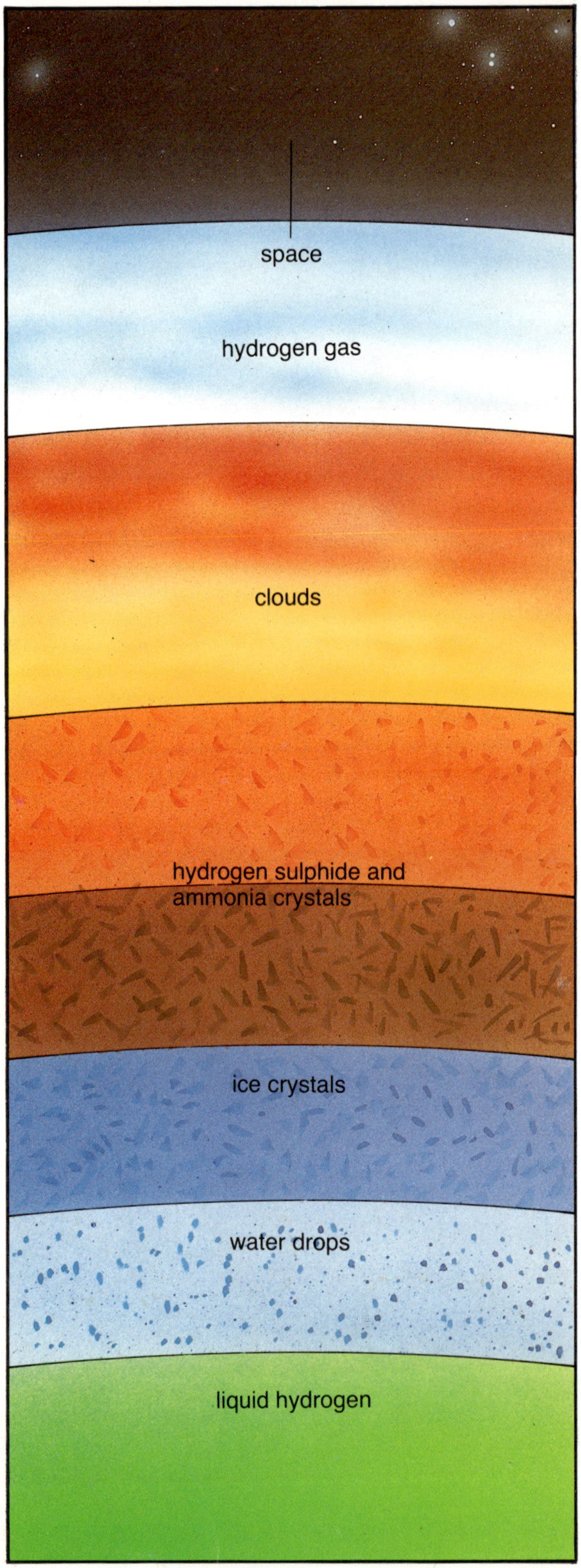

▶ The atmosphere of Jupiter is very cold at the top and hot at the bottom. Its clouds are made up of crystals and droplets of ammonia and hydrogen sulphide, ice crystals and drops of water.

space

hydrogen gas

clouds

hydrogen sulphide and ammonia crystals

ice crystals

water drops

liquid hydrogen

The Great Red Spot

The biggest shape we can see on Jupiter is a huge red oval, three times the size of the Earth. It is called the Great Red Spot. Parts of the spot spin around once in six days. Astronomers first saw the spot through their telescopes 330 years ago. Sometimes the spot fades from view, but it has always returned. It may not last for ever.

The Pioneer and Voyager space probes found that the Great Red Spot is very cold.

This means its top is high up in the atmosphere. The spot spins around in an anti-clockwise direction. It is an enormous whirling storm, a bit like the **hurricanes** we have on Earth. The storm stirs up gases from below. They rise to the top of the atmosphere and form red clouds.

▼ The Great Red Spot is a huge whirling storm in Jupiter's atmosphere. The white oval just above it in this picture is a smaller storm. It is one of three white ovals first seen in 1939.

Jupiter: close neighbours

▶ The icy surface of Europa may cover a layer of water, softer ice or slush. Beneath this is a large rocky core. Sometimes the surface ice cracks open. Water may come up to the surface and freeze.

▲ Before 1979, we did not know that Jupiter is surrounded by a ring of tiny dust particles, rather like those of Saturn. The position of this very faint ring has been drawn on the photograph.

Jupiter's moons

Name	Diameter (km)	Distance from Jupiter (km)
Metis	40	127 600
Adrastea	25	129 000
Amalthea	260	181 300
Thebe	110	225 000
Io	3642	421 600
Europa	3130	670 900
Ganymede	5268	1 070 000
Callisto	4806	1 883 000
Leda	10	11 100 000
Himalia	170	11 470 000
Lysithea	25	11 710 000
Elara	80	11 743 000
Ananke	20	20 700 000
Carme	30	22 350 000
Pasiphaë	40	23 300 000
Sinope	30	23 700 000

Jupiter is not alone in space. It has moons which travel around it, just as our Moon circles the Earth. Jupiter has 16 moons, while Earth has just one. The Voyager space probes found that Jupiter also has a ring around it. Astronomers on Earth could not see the ring through their telescopes because it is very faint. The ring is a thin orange band. It circles Jupiter below the nearest of its moons. It goes right down to the top of the atmosphere.

Jupiter's ring contains specks of dust. Each of these particles moves around the planet like a tiny moon. Some of the particles come from Jupiter's nearer moons. Pieces of rock called **meteorites** travel through space. Sometimes, they hit

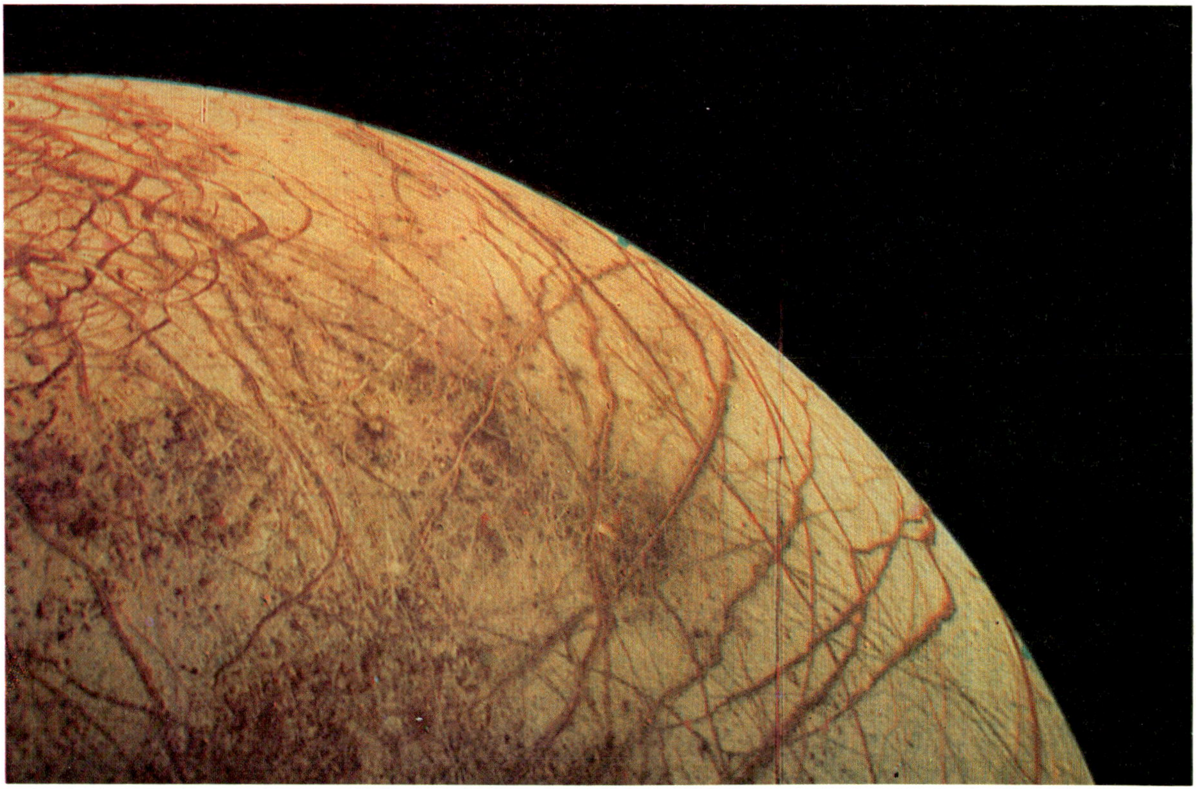

Jupiter's moons. When this happens, pieces of the moons may be knocked off. The pieces join the ring around the planet.

The inner moons

The four moons nearest to Jupiter are all small. Then come four big moons. They were first spotted by the Italian astronomer Galileo Galilei in 1610. You can see them through **binoculars**.

The inner two of these large moons are called Io and Europa. They are about the same size as our Moon, but they are different in every other way. Io is a bright red-orange world with many **volcanoes**. These are mountains that spout out hot yellow **sulphur**. The inside of Io must be so hot that it is liquid. An immense electric current flows through the space between Io and Jupiter.

Europa is as smooth as a billiard ball. It is covered with ice. The surface of Europa is criss-crossed with narrow lines. This suggests that the ice has cracked in places.

▶ The surface of Io is brightly coloured like an Italian pizza. Fountains of sulphur spout from inside Io. Dark streaks of sulphur have flooded parts of the surface.

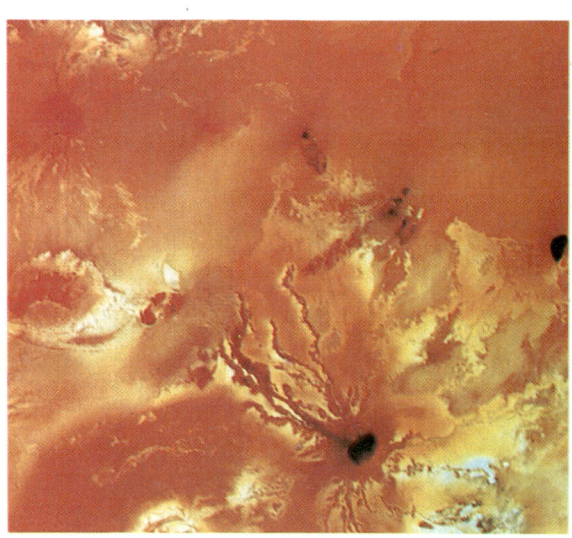

17

Jupiter: the outer moons

The outer two of the big moons which were first seen by Galileo are called Ganymede and Callisto. Ganymede is the largest moon of Jupiter, and it is the biggest moon in the Solar System. It is even larger than the planets Mercury and Pluto.

Ganymede and Callisto

Ganymede and Callisto are not smooth like Io and Europa. They are pitted with saucer-shaped holes called **craters**. These are like the craters on our Moon. Most of the craters were made long ago, soon after the Solar System formed. There were many pieces of rock moving through space at that time. As these meteorites crashed into the planets and their moons, the craters were made.

The surface of Ganymede is made of ice and rock. Much of the ice is dirty because it is mixed with bits of rock which are very old. Large white patches show around some craters. The patches are clean ice thrown out by rocks which have crashed into the moon in more recent times. Parts of Ganymede are covered with strange patterns of grooves. They are long cracks in the surface of the moon. They are caused by movements of the ice or rock.

Callisto also has a surface of dirty ice and rock. It is covered in craters. The Voyager probes spotted a huge region with rings of ridges. It has been called Valhalla. It was formed when a big meteorite struck the surface of the moon. The crash melted some of the ice and made giant ripples, which then froze solid to form the ridges.

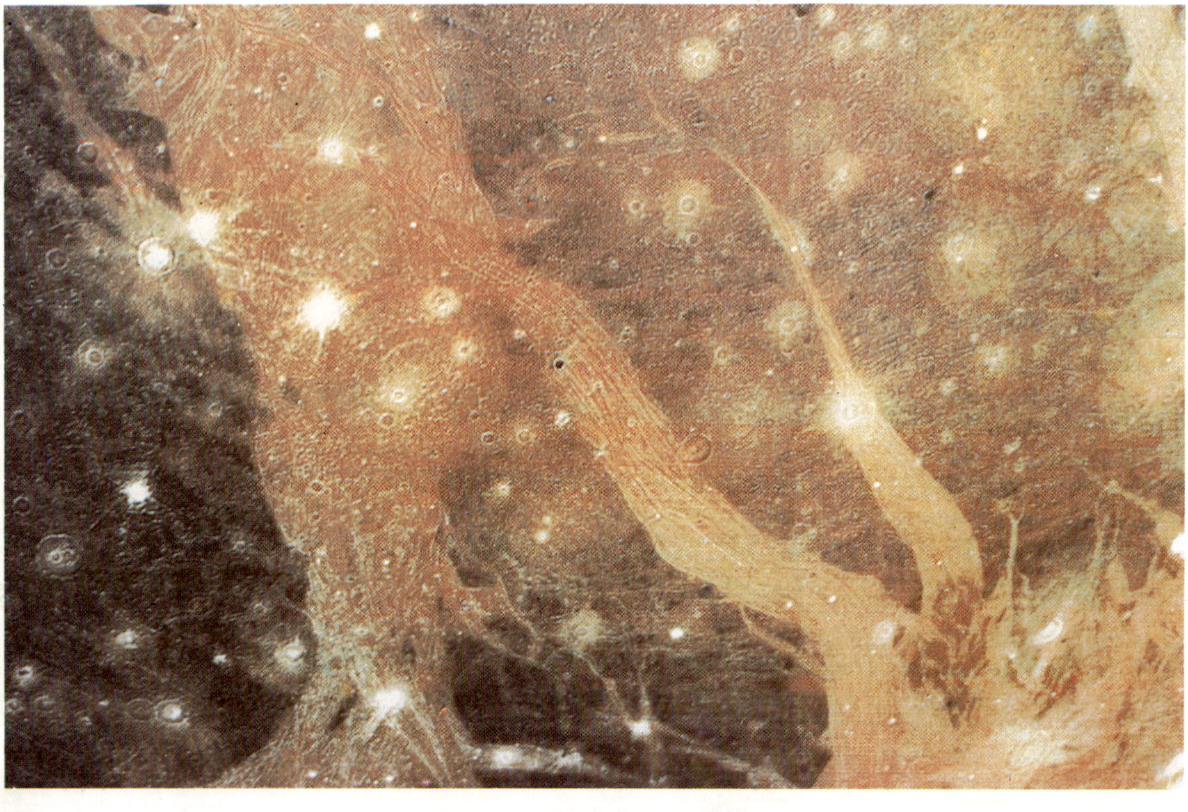

On the outside

Beyond Callisto are two more groups of four moons. All of these are very small. Astronomers on Earth found these eight moons with their telescopes. The Voyager probes did not take pictures of them because they were too far away. Himalia is the only one with a diameter over 150 km. Next in size is Elara with a diameter of 80 km. The others are much smaller.

Of the outside moons, the four that are nearest to Jupiter orbit in the same direction as the planet spins. The outer group of moons travel around Jupiter the other way. This is very unusual. There are only two other moons in the Solar System that move like this.

The eight outer moons are probably pieces of one or more larger bodies that broke up following a collison. They were captured by Jupiter's gravity and stayed in orbit around the planet.

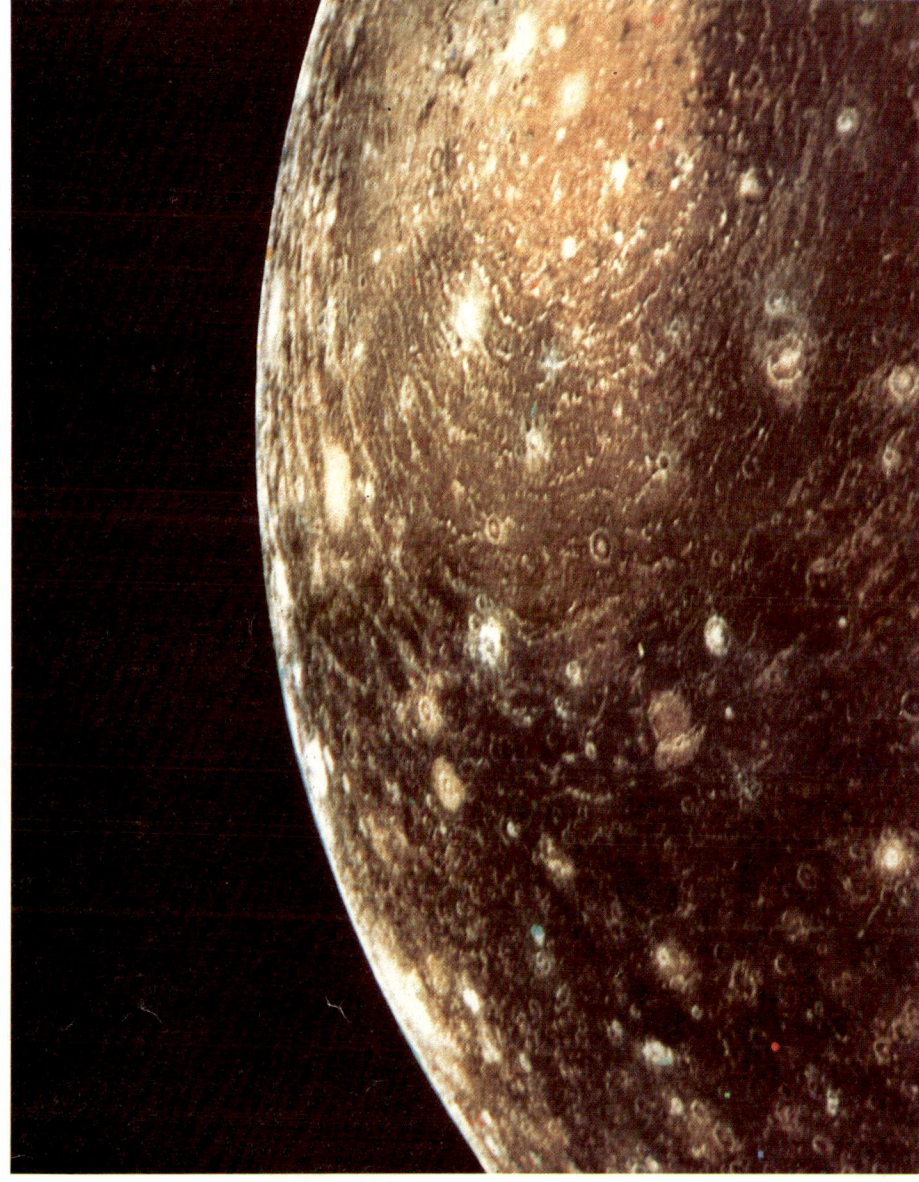

► The rings of the huge area known as Valhalla show where a huge meteorite crashed onto the surface of Callisto long ago. The central part of Valhalla is about 600 km across. The ripples caused by the impact stretch in all directions for about 1500 km from the centre.

◄ Much of the surface of Ganymede is pitted with many small craters. In other places the surface is covered with bundles of long grooves or furrows. These show that the surface of this huge moon is slowly shifting causing it to become buckled and cracked.

Jupiter: the Galileo probe

The most advanced space probe ever built is on its way to explore Jupiter. It is called Galileo, after the man who first saw the four largest moons of Jupiter.

A double mission

Launched in October 1989, Galileo will take just over six years to reach Jupiter. On its way Galileo flies past Venus once, the Earth twice and a couple of **asteroids**, taking many photographs. The asteroids are small planets. They are mainly found between Mars and Jupiter.

Galileo is really two space probes in one. About 150 days before Galileo reaches Jupiter, it will split in two. One part, called the probe, will head straight for Jupiter itself. It will enter Jupiter's atmosphere at over 180 000 km an hour. The probe will be protected from the terrific heat as it slows down by a thick **heat shield**. Then the shield will drop away.

The probe will float down by **parachute** through Jupiter's colourful clouds. For about 90 minutes it will detect the gases in the clouds. It will also measure the changing temperature and pressure. Eventually it will be crushed out of existence. As it descends the probe will radio its results to the other part of Galileo, called the **orbiter**. This will send them on to Earth.

The Galileo orbiter will go into orbit around Jupiter. As it circles the planet again and again it will fly past all the large moons and send back pictures. It will also measure Jupiter's magnetic field. The orbiter should work for two years.

▶ The US Galileo probe separates from the orbiter as they speed towards Jupiter.

Saturn: planet of beauty

Saturn is a special planet. It is surrounded by wide rings which make it the most beautiful planet in the Solar System. Other planets have rings, but none are as big or bright as those of Saturn. Saturn has at least 18 moons and possibly 23, more than any other planet.

Saturn is a large planet. It is second only to Jupiter in size. It spins quickly, too, and this makes the planet bulge around its middle just like Jupiter.

Saturn can be seen in the night sky. It looks like a bright star. You have to use a telescope to spot the rings. Pioneer 11 and both Voyager space probes flew past Saturn. They sent back many clear photographs.

Inside the planet

Apart from its wide rings, Saturn looks very like Jupiter. Bands of storm clouds circle the planet. They move much faster than those on Jupiter. Near the equator strong winds blow from the west at speeds of over 1700 km an hour.

The clouds are made up of coloured layers. The colours are not as bright as those on Jupiter. This is because the atmosphere is very hazy. The bands contain some large spots. One reddish cloud is called Big Bertha! None of the spots is as big as Jupiter's Great Red Spot.

Beneath the clouds, Saturn is like Jupiter, with layers of liquid hydrogen and the peculiar liquid metallic hydrogen. It has a rocky core about the size of the Earth. Saturn is made mostly of hydrogen, the lightest gas. Saturn is less **dense** than any other planet. Its contents are not so closely packed together. If you could put Saturn into a vast ocean of water, it would float!

Through the first telescopes, early drawings of Saturn made by Galileo and other astronomers of the time made it look like three planets close together. In 1655, a Dutchman called Christiaan Huyghens realized the truth. Saturn is surrounded by a thin, flat ring.

Facts about Saturn

Diameter	120 000 km
Mass	95 times that of Earth
Distance from the Sun	1427 million km
Period of rotation	10 hours, 15 minutes
Period of revolution	29.5 years
Tilt of axis	27°
Gravity on the surface	1.2 times that of Earth
Temperature of cloud tops	− 180°C
Atmosphere	hydrogen, helium
Number of moons	possibly 23

Earth   Saturn

Saturn's path through space

Saturn's rings can often be seen clearly through a telescope, but sometimes they seem to vanish. This is because of the tilt of Saturn's axis.

Saturn takes nearly 30 years to go once around the Sun. As it moves, our view of the planet changes. During part of its orbit, the planet appears to be tilted over. The top or the bottom half faces towards us. In between, it seems to straighten up.

When the planet is tilted over, we can see the whole of the rings. When the planet is straight, we look at the rings edge-on. The rings are very thin, and they seem to vanish from our view.

▶ The two Voyager space probes took many photographs of Saturn and its rings. They showed up the light and dark bands in the planet's atmosphere. These show the gases in the different cloud layers. The markings on Saturn were not as obvious as those on Jupiter. They were hidden by haze.

Saturn: the rings

When we look through telescopes at Saturn, we can see three broad rings around it.

The rings are not solid. The planet can be seen through them. The rings are made up of many pieces of ice, moving in circles around Saturn like tiny moons. Some pieces are smaller than grains of sand. Others are giant icy boulders, as big as a house.

The outer ring we can see is called the A ring. Then we see a dark gap. The gap is called the Cassini Division. It is named after the Italian astronomer Giovanni Cassini, who first saw it in 1675. Then, there is a central ring called the B ring. The ring which looks as if it is on the inside is called the C ring. It is fainter than the other two.

Photographs from Pioneer and Voyager showed up even more rings. There is an inner D ring which is very faint. There are also two narrow outer rings called the F and G rings. Beyond these is a wide but faint E ring. In all, the rings are about 480 000 km across.

Icy circles

The Voyager photographs showed that the main rings contain thousands of narrow **ringlets**, or smaller rings, and many gaps. There are even ringlets in Cassini's Division. The rings are very thin. The B ring is the thickest. It is only 100 to 150 metres thick. The A and C rings are just a few tens of metres thick. This explains why they almost disappear when seen edge on.

How and when were the rings formed? Perhaps they were made when one of Saturn's moons broke up near the planet, pulled apart by Saturn's gravity after straying too close. Or maybe it was smashed to pieces after colliding with another body. The pieces spread out into a broad ring around the planet. Today many people think the rings are as old as Saturn itself. The planet formed from gas and dust in space. The rings were the icy pieces left over after the planet formed.

Voyager also spotted mysterious dark marks in the rings, rotating like the spokes of a wheel. These patterns may be caused by Saturn's magnetic field.

▼ The rings of Saturn have different colours. For this photograph a computer has been used to strengthen the colours. This helps us to see them more clearly. Astronomers are not sure why the rings are coloured in this way. Perhaps the ice which makes up the rings is not pure. Saturn's rings are the finest in the Solar System.

Saturn: the inner moons

Before 1980, people thought that Saturn had ten moons. Then the Voyager probes found several more. We now know that Saturn has at least 18 moons and maybe as many as 23. We know very little about some of the smaller moons.

Saturn's inner moons		
Name	Diameter (km)	Distance from Saturn (km)
(A ring gap)	20	133 400
Atlas	35	137 670
Prometheus	145	139 350
Pandora	110	141 700
Janus	195	151 420
Epimetheus	140	151 470
Mimas	398	185 600
Enceladus	498	238 100
Tethys	1046	294 700
Telesto	30	294 700
Calypso	30	294 700
Dione	1120	377 500
Helene	35	378 060
Rhea	1528	527 200

▼ Dione is one of Saturn's icy inner moons. It is one-third the size of Earth's Moon and it is covered with craters. There are a few large craters but most are less than 40 km across.

▶ A photograph taken by Voyager 2 shows Enceladus, another of the inner moons of Saturn. It is made of ice and rock, but its surface is different from that of the other icy moons. Only part is scarred with craters. Elsewhere the surface is smooth, with some narrow ridges.

The inner moons are mainly made up of ice, mixed with a little rock. They are covered with craters and cracks. The nearest moon, which has no name, lies in a gap in the A ring. Next comes Atlas, just outside the A ring. Prometheus and Pandora are called shepherd moons. They orbit on either side of the narrow F ring. Their gravity makes the ringlets in the F ring twist like strands of rope.

Janus and Epimetheus have orbits which are almost the same. They swap orbits with each other from time to time. Tethys, Telesto and Calypso all move in the same orbit around Saturn. They travel ahead of or behind each other. They do not collide.

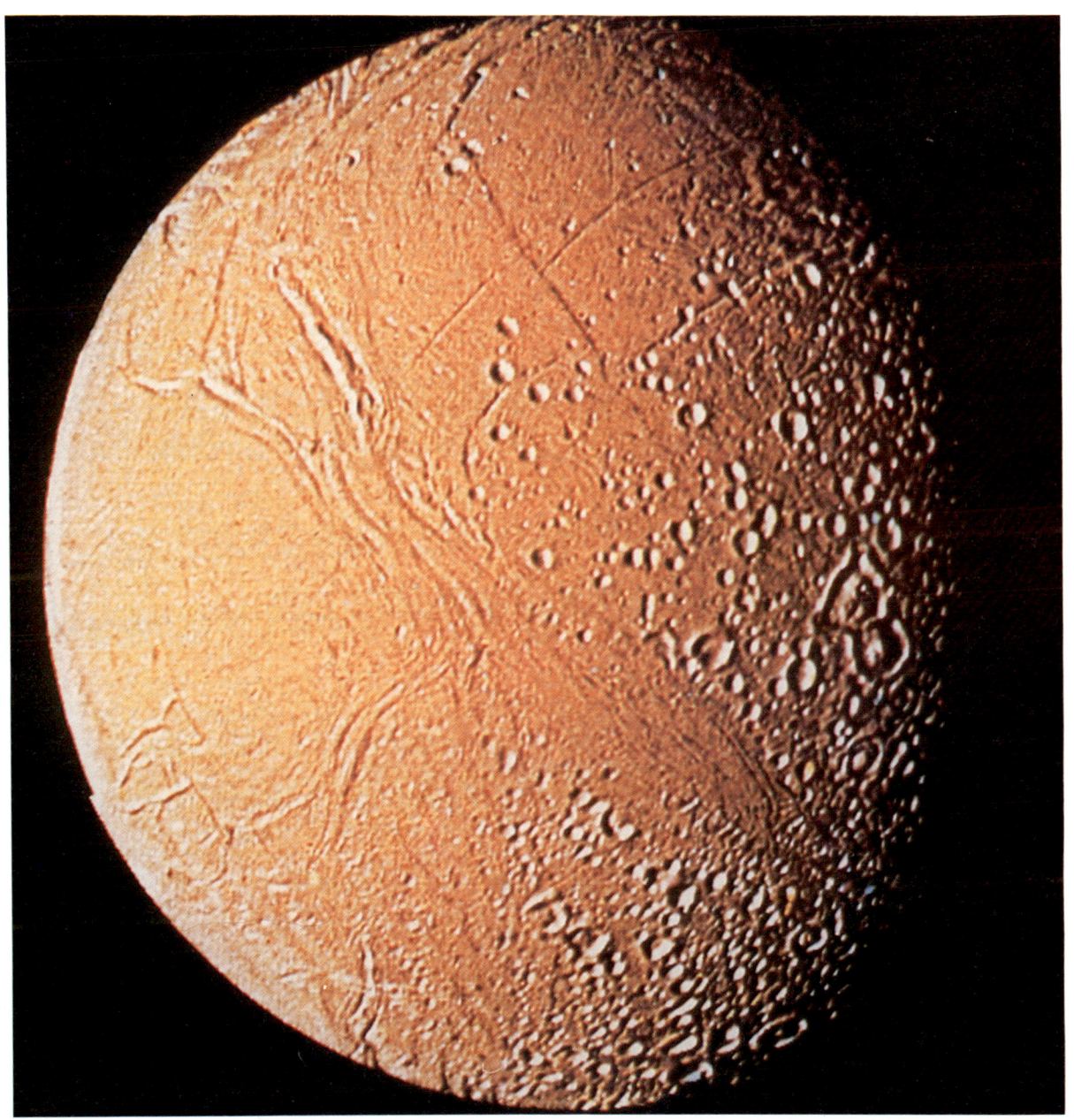

Saturn: the outer moons

▼ The orange fog around Titan was photographed by Voyager 1. The surface of this large moon lies hidden from sight. Titan is bigger than the planets Mercury and Pluto.

The first of Saturn's outer moons is called Titan. It is the second biggest moon in the Solar System. Titan has an atmosphere. It is very unusual for a moon to be surrounded by a layer of gas like a planet is. Voyager 1 took a close look at Titan when it flew past Saturn in 1980.

A hidden world

The photographs that came back showed a world covered in an orange fog. The surface could not be seen at all. The atmosphere contains mostly the gas **nitrogen**, which is also the main gas in the Earth's atmosphere. On Earth we have **oxygen** as well, but Titan has none. Instead, it has **methane**. This is the natural gas which we use for heating on Earth.

The fog is caused by drops of orange liquid in the atmosphere of Titan. The coloured liquid is made when rays from the Sun strike the gases. The surface of Titan is very cold. It is thought the surface may be covered by oceans of liquid methane, or perhaps brown snow made of methane. The inside of Titan is made of ice with a core of rock.

A European probe called Huyghens, carried to Saturn by the Cassini probe, will parachute into Titan's atmosphere early in the next century. Long ago the Earth may have been like Titan is now. Titan may help us find out how life began on Earth.

Facts about Titan	
Diameter	5150 km
Distance from Saturn	1 221 600 km
Surface temperature	−180°C
Pressure of atmosphere	1.6 times Earth
Period of rotation and revolution	15.9 days
Gravity on the surface	⅙ of Earth

▲ Iapetus is a world of dark and light rock. It orbits Saturn at a distance of about 3½ million km. It is less than one-third the size of Titan, and is pitted with craters.

On the edge

Beyond Titan are three more moons. First comes Hyperion. This is a small world mainly made of ice, with light and dark areas on its surface. Hyperion is very irregular in shape. It may have collided with another body in the past.

Beyond Hyperion is Iapetus. This strange moon is dark on one side and light on the other. The dark material may have come out from the inside of the moon. The outermost moon is called Phoebe. It goes around Saturn the opposite way to all the other moons. Phoebe may be an asteroid that was captured by the pull of Saturn's gravity.

Saturn's outer moons		
Name	Diameter (km)	Distance from Saturn (km)
Hyperion	360	1 483 000
Iapetus	1436	3 560 000
Phoebe	220	12 950 000

Uranus: the tilted planet

The next of the outer planets lies beyond Saturn. It is called Uranus. It is so faint that it can only just be seen from Earth without a telescope. People used to think that it was a star. In 1781, William Herschel used a telescope to find out that Uranus is a planet. He saw a green disc with no markings on it.

Uranus is the third largest planet in the Solar System. Astronomers later spotted five moons. In 1977, Uranus was found to have rings. Even so, using the biggest telescopes they had, astronomers could not find out very much about the planet itself.

In 1986, the space probe Voyager 2 flew past Uranus. It sent back very clear photographs of the planet and its rings and moons. At last, we could find out more about Uranus.

Inside Uranus

The probe's photographs of Uranus explained why astronomers could see so little. The whole planet is covered by a layer of blue-green haze. Voyager spotted a few clouds beneath the haze. They showed winds blowing from the west at speeds up to 580 km an hour. The atmosphere contains mainly the gases hydrogen and helium with some methane.

Beneath the atmosphere is a layer of gas and icy materials, then a layer containing mixtures of gas, ice and rock. A small core of hot rock may exist at the centre of the planet.

Sideways on

Uranus is a very unusual planet. It spins about an axis which leans over so far, that Uranus is lying on its side. No other planet is like this. Uranus also has a strong magnetic field. This too is tilted, but away from the axis around which the planet spins. No one knows why this is so. Long ago Uranus may have been struck by a large asteroid which turned it over.

As Uranus goes around the Sun, first one pole and then the other points towards the Sun. Each pole and the region around it is in daylight for 42 years. Then it spends the next 42 years in darkness. Voyager found that the dark pole has the same temperature as the pole that is in sunlight. This was also surprising.

Facts about Uranus	
Diameter	51 120 km
Mass	15 times that on Earth
Distance from the Sun	2870 million km
Period of rotation	17 hours, 15 minutes
Period of revolution	84 years
Tilt of axis	98°
Gravity on the surface	9/10 of that on Earth
Temperature of cloud tops	−210°C
Atmosphere	hydrogen, helium, methane
Moons	15

Earth   Uranus

The Earth is only slightly tilted as it orbits the Sun, but Uranus travels on its side. This diagram shows the orbit of Uranus between the years 1966 and 2029. The planet's tilted orbit means that from Earth we can see its north and south poles as well as its equator.

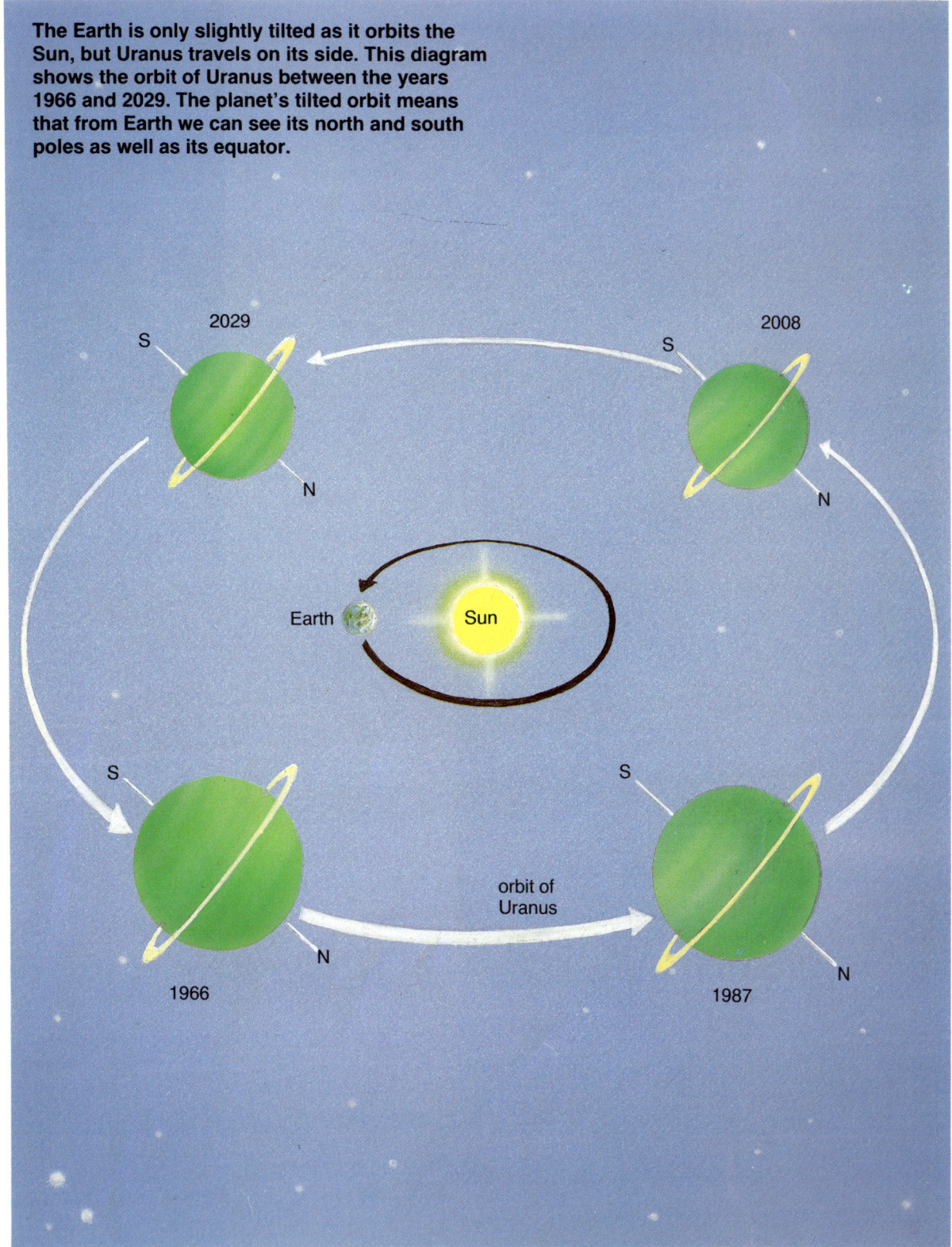

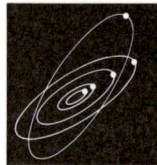

Uranus: rings and moons

The rings of Uranus are very dark. Unlike the bright rings of Saturn, they do not show up in telescopes. The rings of Uranus were spotted by an **airborne observatory** in 1977. This is a special aircraft that carries a telescope. Astronomers on the plane were watching Uranus as it passed by a star. The star blinked on and off as the planet's rings moved in front of it.

◀ Uranus and its rings, as they might appear from its moon Miranda. The rings appear as a thin line because they are seen edge on. A blue-green haze covers the planet. It reflects the light from the Sun.

▲ The rings of Uranus may look like this when seen in close-up. Countless dark pieces of ice travel around the planet.

Dark ice

Voyager 2 looked at the rings as it flew past Uranus. It found 11 rings and parts of several others. Rings are circular. The rings are thin, very dark and narrow. The broadest ring is less than 100 km wide. Between the rings are wide gaps full of hundreds of ringlets of very fine dust.

The main rings of Uranus are made of many very dark, icy boulders moving around the planet. The ice may be frozen methane. If the icy boulders crash into each other, this could make lots of fine dust. This would collect in the gaps between the rings.

Strange moons

Voyager also spotted ten small moons around Uranus which had not been seen before. All are in orbit between the rings and Miranda. Miranda is the nearest of the five moons that were already known. The moons of Uranus are made up of rock and ice.

Miranda is one of the oddest moons in the Solar System. Its surface is scarred by craters, valleys and cliffs. On Miranda, there are cliffs of ice 5 km high! Some astronomers think Miranda may once have broken apart. Later, the pieces came back together again. Another moon, Umbriel is very dark. The other three large moons are brighter and icy, with big dark patches.

The larger moons of Uranus		
Name	**Diameter (km)**	**Distance from Uranus (km)**
Miranda	472	129 400
Ariel	1158	191 000
Umbriel	1169	266 300
Titania	1578	435 000
Oberon	1523	583 000

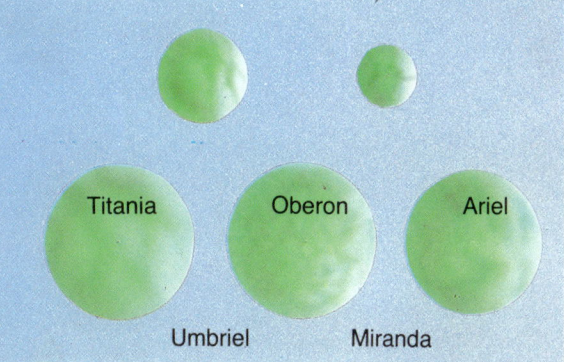

Neptune: the blue planet

Once Uranus was discovered, people measured its path through space. The planet did not move as expected. Some people worked out that another big planet must exist. This unknown planet would lie beyond Uranus. Its gravity would pull at Uranus and so change its orbit.

In 1845, two astronomers in Britain and France worked out where the new planet ought to be seen. They both agreed. Others began to look for the new planet. In 1846, a German called Johann Galle spotted the new world with his telescope. It was exactly where the others had said it would be. The new planet looked blue, and it was called Neptune. Neptune was named after the Roman god of the sea.

A distant world

Neptune is almost as large as Uranus. It is the fourth biggest planet in the Solar System. It is so far away from Earth that it appears very faint. The planet cannot be seen with the naked eye, but you can spot it with binoculars. It looks like a star. Only one spacecraft has so far visited Neptune. Voyager 2 flew past the planet in August 1989. It made many exciting discoveries.

The blue giant

Voyager's photographs showed that Neptune is deep blue in colour. The atmosphere contains the gases hydrogen and helium, with a little methane. The methane gives Neptune its blue colour. Many wispy clouds could be seen. These clouds are made of crystals of methane ice.

Voyager also found a large, grey oval spot. It is called the Great Dark Spot. It is rather like Jupiter's Great Red Spot. The Great Dark Spot may be a huge whirling storm in Neptune's atmosphere.

There are violent winds on Neptune. Most winds blow from the east to west. This is opposite to the rotation of the planet. The strongest winds, near the Great Dark Spot, blow at over 1200 km an hour. These are the strongest westward blowing winds of any planet, including windy Saturn.

Neptune has a weak magnetic field. This is tilted away from the axis around which the planet spins. So, surprisingly, Neptune's magnetic field is rather like that of Uranus.

Facts about Neptune

Diameter	50 540 km
Mass	17 times that of Earth
Distance from the Sun	4497 million km
Period of rotation	16 hours, 3 minutes
Period of revolution	164.8 years
Tilt of axis	29°
Gravity on the surface	1.2 times that of Earth
Temperature of cloud tops	−220°C
Atmosphere	hydrogen, helium, methane
Moons	8

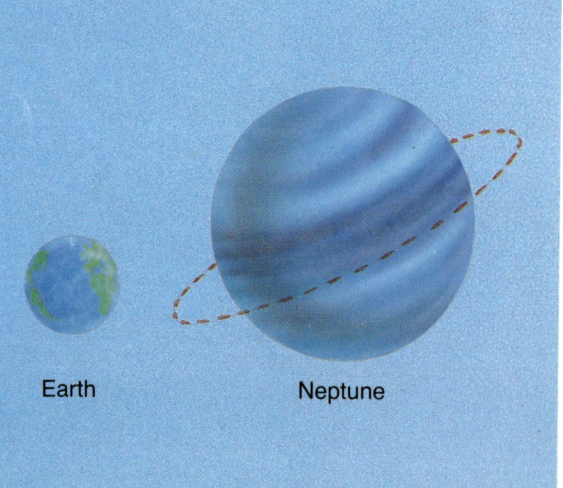

Earth   Neptune

▼ This painting shows the US space probe Voyager 2 after it swooped just 5000 km above the north pole of Neptune in August 1989.

Neptune: rings and moons

Voyager showed us that Neptune has rings. They go all the way round the planet. There are two narrow rings and a wider ring closer in. These rings contain very dark icy boulders. There is also a broad sheet of tiny dust particles outside the inner narrow ring. In the main rings the particles fill only one tenth of the total space. Neptune's rings are very flimsy indeed.

Before Voyager 2 flew by, astronomers knew of two moons around Neptune. Tiny Nereid is just 340 km across. As it goes around Neptune its distance varies from 1 353 600 km to 9 623 700 km. Voyager showed us that the other moon, Triton, is 2700 km across. This was smaller than expected. Triton has more rock and less ice than the small moons of Saturn. Triton circles Neptune at a distance of 355 300 km.

The cold pink moon

Triton is the coldest place ever visited by a space probe. Its surface temperature is − 236°C. The surface is a mixture of nitrogen and methane ices, frozen as hard as rock. Near the south pole is a layer of pink snow. Further north the ice is thick and dark red in colour. Triton also has exploding ice fountains on its surface.

Triton circles its planet the other way to most moons. Long ago Triton may have moved around the Sun on its own. Then it was captured by the pull of Neptune's gravity.

Voyager found six new moons around Neptune. One is bigger than Nereid. It is as dark as soot and unevenly shaped.

Voyager 2 flies past Neptune and approaches Triton. The probe will send back pictures of this large moon.

◄ The southern half of Neptune's largest moon, Triton, is bright and covered in what appears to be pink snow. The northern half is darker and covered in a sheet of ice. Triton is the coldest place spacecraft have so far visited in our Solar System.

▲ A close-up view of
Neptune's mysterious Great
Dark Spot, which is as large
as our planet Earth. Scientists
think that the spot is a huge
storm system spinning in an
anti-clockwise direction.

Pluto: the ninth planet

When Neptune was discovered, people thought the Solar System was complete. But Uranus and Neptune still did not move as expected. Perhaps there was another planet beyond Neptune still to be discovered. It might be the gravity of this planet that was pulling the other planets out of position. A search was started for a ninth planet in the Solar System.

This new planet was discovered in 1930. An American called Clyde Tombaugh spotted it in photographs of the sky. The planet was called Pluto. It can only be seen through a big telescope.

Most of the time, Pluto is the farthest planet from the Sun. During part of its orbit, it comes nearer to the Sun than Neptune. It is in this part of its orbit now. It will become the most distant planet again in 1999.

The frozen planet

Pluto is a tiny world. It is smaller than any other planet. It is even smaller than our Moon. It is very cold. Pluto has a very thin atmosphere of methane gas. Some astronomers think that this atmosphere may only appear when Pluto is nearest to the Sun. The surface could be covered in a layer of methane ice.

We think that Pluto is made of ice with a large core of rock. The rock probably makes up three-quarters of the total.

Pluto's moon

Pluto has a moon called Charon. It was first seen through a telescope in 1978. Charon is about 1200 km across. This is roughly half the size of Pluto.

Charon orbits the planet at a distance of 19 400 km. It takes the same time to go around Pluto as Pluto takes to spin once on its axis. From the surface of Pluto, Charon would appear fixed in the sky. From one side of Pluto, Charon may always be seen. From the other side of Pluto, Charon can never be seen. Unlike Pluto, Charon may be covered in a layer of water ice.

Pluto and Charon are an odd pair. None of the present space probes will go near them. For now there are no plans to send a space probe to Pluto and Charon. Perhaps a space probe will go there early on in the next century.

Facts about Pluto	
Diameter	2245 km
Mass	1/500 that of Earth
Distance from the Sun	5900 million km
Period of rotation	6 days, 9 hours, 18 minutes
Period or revolution	248.5 years
Tilt of axis	118°
Gravity on the surface	1/16 that of Earth
Surface temperature	−215°C
Atmosphere	methane
Moons	1

Earth   Pluto

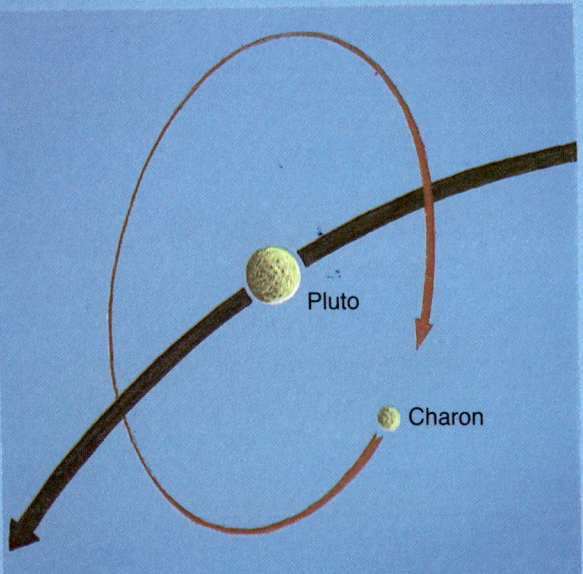

▲ As Pluto orbits the Sun, it is circled by a moon called Charon. Charon is about one-third the size of the Earth's Moon.

Pluto travels through the outer regions of the Solar System. It is always so far from the Sun, that it can only ever receive about $1/2000$ of the heat and light from the Sun that we receive on Earth. That is why Pluto is so bitterly cold.

Planet X?

The Solar System has nine planets that we know about. Some people think that there could be a tenth planet that has not yet been found. It is often called Planet X. The Roman number for ten is X, but X can also mean something that is not known.

Why are people looking for a tenth planet? When Pluto was found, astronomers thought that it would be the missing planet that pulled at the orbits of Uranus and Neptune with its gravity. It is not. Pluto is too small to do this. Out in space, there may still be a missing planet, Planet X.

▲ This machine was put into orbit around Earth in 1983. It was called IRAS, the Infra-Red Astronomy Satellite. It looked for heat rays coming from space. Planets reflect heat from the Sun, and some make their own heat. IRAS might have picked up heat coming from Planet X.

If Planet X exists, it should be in a distant orbit far beyond Pluto. After finding Pluto in 1930, Clyde Tombaugh continued his hunt for distant planets. He examined photographs showing over 90 million stars. He did not find another planet. So Planet X must be very faint indeed. It will be very difficult to find.

▲ Signals from distant space probes are picked up at Goldstone, California, in the United States. The signals might give us a clue about whether Planet X exists or not.

The search

Astronomers are now searching for Planet X. How could they find it? The four Pioneer and Voyager space probes are moving beyond the outer planets. They could be tugged at by the gravity of Planet X. If any probe wanders off its expected path, it might tell us roughly where the missing planet is.

Photographs of the sky could also show up Planet X. Machines called **satellites** are put into orbit around Earth. Some of them search the sky. Photographs taken by a satellite called IRAS in 1983 and 1984 might show it. This satellite has mapped thousands of objects in the sky which give off heat. One of them could turn out to be Planet X.

Since 1910 the outer planets have moved as expected. Some astronomers think Planet X does not exist. Others think the path of Planet X is tilted to that of the other planets. Its gravity may not be pulling on the outer planets as much as it used to.

Snowballs in space

We have now looked at all the outer planets and their moons. But there are other strange objects in the outer Solar System. One of these is called Chiron. Discovered in 1977, it looked like an asteroid about 300 km across. It moves in the space between Saturn and Uranus. In 1989, astronomers found an atmosphere around Chiron. It may be rocky or icy. Nobody knows what it is. Some think it was once a moon of Saturn.

There are other unusual objects beyond Pluto. They are like large dirty snowballs. There could be millions of them floating in a huge cloud that surrounds the whole Solar System.

Beautiful tails

Sometimes, the gravity of a passing star pulls at the cloud of snowballs. Some of them begin to move in towards the Sun. If they come close enough to the Sun, the ice in the snowball heats up. Gas and dust spurt out and form a fuzzy cloud around the snowball and a long tail. This is called a **comet**.

A comet does not usually fall into the Sun. It swings around the Sun and heads back into space. Often it never returns. Sometimes a planet's gravity changes its path. The comet is pulled into orbit around the Sun.

We may see a comet if it comes near Earth. The tail may be bright. It may be seen in the night sky for some weeks.

▼ Comet West could be seen from Earth in 1976. Its tail was streaming outwards as it neared the Sun. It was made of dust and gas.

Bits and pieces

As a comet flies away from the Sun, it cools. The tail shrinks and disappears. The comet leaves a trail of dust behind it in space.

As the Earth moves around the Sun, it crosses some of these dust trails. It passes through each one at the same time each year. When this happens, we may see lots of **meteors**. These are bits of dust that strike the Earth's atmosphere at high speed. They burn up in a streak of light. We call these streaks **shooting stars**.

A comet loses a lot of gas and dust each time it goes around the Sun. After many visits, it may have none left. It disappears.

▶ A comet glows faintly in the evening sky. A few comets that pass close by our Earth are among the brightest objects we can see in the sky. Brilliant comets like this are rare. You might see only one or two in a lifetime.

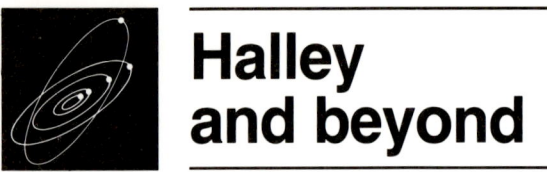

Halley and beyond

The orbit of Halley's comet led it past the Earth in 1986. As the comet returns to the more distant parts of the Solar System, it loses its long tail.

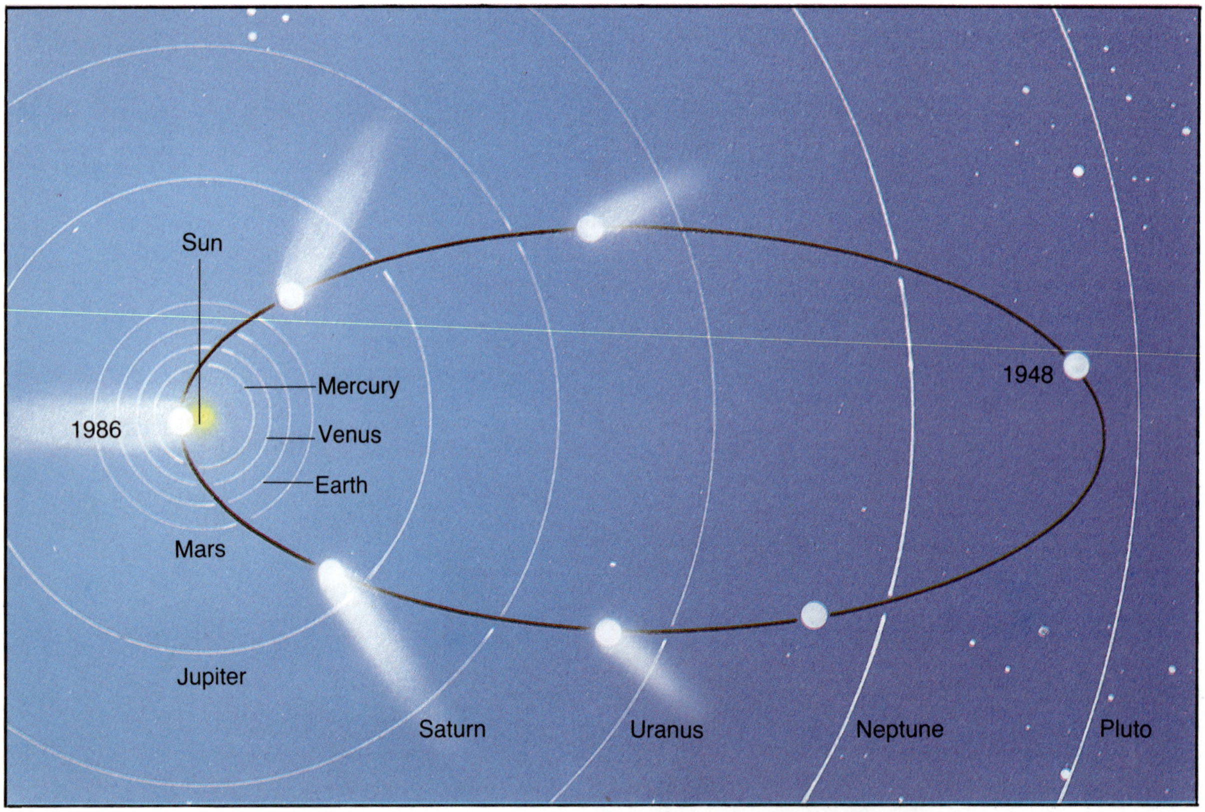

Sun

Mercury

Venus

Earth

1986

Mars

Jupiter

1948

Saturn

Uranus

Neptune

Pluto

The most famous comet is Halley's comet. It is named after a British astronomer, Edmond Halley. He saw it in 1682. In 1705, Halley worked out that this comet returns every 76 years. In between, it moves out beyond Neptune.

Halley calculated that the comet would next be seen in 1758. The comet returned on time. Halley's comet has come back every 76 years since then. The last time was in 1986. It will be seen again in the year 2061.

People had seen Halley's comet long before Halley. The Chinese first wrote about the comet in 240 B.C.

Into the comet

Space probes were sent to look at Halley's comet in 1986. One of these was called Giotto. It reached a speed of 250 000 km an hour as it sped past the comet.

Giotto sent back pictures of the dust and ice ball at the heart of the comet. This is called the **nucleus**. It is 16 km long and shaped like a pear. Giotto had a shield to protect it from bits of dust hitting it at tremendous speed.

Jets of gas and dust spurt from the nucleus. The surface is a layer of dark dust, blacker than coal. Inside is snow and ice mixed with dust and some rock.

▼ The Giotto probe flew close to Halley's comet in 1986. It came within 600 km of the comet's nucleus. Giotto was launched by ESA, the European Space Agency.

Beyond the comet cloud

Our space probes take years to reach the outer planets. The distances are vast. Yet even the farthest planet is a thousand times nearer to us than the comets in the comet cloud. The edge of the cloud is far away from Earth. Yet the cloud is less than half way to Proxima Centauri, the nearest star to our Sun.

When we explore the outer planets, we are only taking a small step out into the Universe. Beyond the Solar System lie thousands of millions of stars. Many of the stars must have planets of their own. We have found out all kinds of facts about the planets in our own Solar System. Out in the Universe there must be many more marvels and new worlds to explore.

Glossary

airborne observatory: an aircraft fitted with telescopes and other equipment for the study of space

ammonia: a kind of gas which has a very strong smell and no colour

asteroids: mini-planets travelling around the Sun, mainly between the orbits of Mars and Jupiter.

astrologer: someone who believes that the stars and planets have an effect on the lives of people who live on Earth

astronomer: someone who studies the stars and planets and other objects in space

atmosphere: the layer of gases which surrounds a planet or a star. The Earth's atmosphere is the air

axis: an imaginary straight line from the top to the bottom of a spinning object, such as a planet. The object turns or rotates around this line

binoculars: a kind of double telescope with two eyepieces

comet: a small icy body in the Solar System. When near the Sun, the ice heats up. Gas and dust spurt out. These spread out making the comet's fuzzy head and long tail.

computer: a machine which uses electric power for collecting, sorting and storing information very quickly

core: the centre of something

crater: a bowl-shaped hollow. There are many craters on some planets and moons

crystal: any substance which has a solid shape made up of angled patterns. Ice is formed from crystals

dense: having its contents packed closely together, so that even a small piece is very heavy.

diameter: the width of a circle or sphere. This is measured from one point on the outside, through the centre, to a point on the opposite side

dust: tiny pieces of solid matter. A lot of dust floats around in space

Earth: our home planet, the third planet in order of increasing distance from the Sun.

electric current: a flow of electricity. It can pass along metals and other materials

equator: an imaginary line passing around the middle of a planet or star. It is halfway between the two poles

gas: a light substance that is neither liquid nor solid. Air is made up of several gases

gravity: the force that pulls objects towards each other. The Sun's gravity keeps the Earth in orbit around it. The Earth's gravity keeps us on the Earth. Gravity makes objects fall and gives them weight

heat shield: a thick layer of special material built around a spacecraft to protect it from heat. When spacecraft enter the atmosphere of a planet, they become very hot. The heat shield stops them burning up

helium: a gas which is the second lightest substance in the Universe

hurricanes: enormous swirling storms. On Earth, the winds in a hurricane blow at speeds of 120 km an hour or more.

hydrogen: the lightest substance in the Universe

hydrogen sulphide: a colourless gas which smells like rotten eggs

magnet: a piece of metal that can attract some metal objects towards it or force them away

magnetic field: the region of force around a magnet

mass: the amount of matter in an object. Mass is not affected by gravity. It does not change if the object is on the Earth or in space. It is different from weight which is affected by gravity

meteor: a small piece of rock or dust from space which burns up as it strikes the layer of gases around the Earth. As it burns it makes a streak of light in the sky.

meteorite: a piece of rock and metal from space which manages to pass through a planet's atmosphere without burning up. It crashes onto the surface of the planet forming a crater. Meteorites also crash into moons.

methane: a colourless gas which can burn. It is found underground on Earth, and is present on many planets

moon: a smaller body that travels around a planet. The planet Jupiter has 16 moons. The Earth has only one Moon. Our Moon is a small world with no atmosphere and no life

nitrogen: a gas found in the atmosphere of some planets. It has no colour, smell or taste. It does not burn

nucleus: the central part of an object such as a comet

orbit: a path through space made by one thing going around another. The planets move in orbit around the Sun

orbiter: part of a space probe which goes into orbit around a planet

oxygen: a gas found in air. Oxygen is very important to all plants and animals. We cannot breathe without oxygen

parachute: something which helps a heavy object float to the ground. Spacecraft sometimes use parachutes when landing on a planet which has an atmosphere

particle: a tiny speck of solid matter

period of revolution: the time it takes for a planet or other object to travel once around another object

period of rotation: the time it takes for a planet or other body to spin once on its axis.

planet: a body in space which moves around a star like the Sun. The planet shines by reflecting the light of the star

pole: the most northern or southern point on a star, planet or moon

pressure: the action of one thing pressing on or against something else. The atmosphere of a planet presses against the surface

radio signal: a message sent by using invisible waves that travel through the air or space

ring: a band of rock, ice, dust or frozen gas circling a planet

ringlet: a narrow band of rock, ice, dust or frozen gas circling around a planet. Often many ringlets make up a single ring

rocket: something which burns fuel to make it move forwards or upwards very quickly. Rockets are cylinder-shaped and are used for fireworks, signals, and for launching spacecraft

satellite: a small body in orbit around a larger body in space. Io is a satellite of Jupiter. We also call spacecraft that orbit the Earth satellites

shooting star: the streak of light seen when a meteor enters the Earth's atmosphere and burns up

Solar System: The Sun, and all the objects that orbit it, such as planets and their moons

space probe: a machine sent from Earth to study objects in space. It does not have people on board

star: a glowing ball of gas that gives off its own light and heat. The Sun is a star

sulphur: a yellow, solid substance that is found in the Earth and other bodies in the Solar System. It burns with a blue flame

Sun: the star nearest to the Earth. It gives us all our light and heat

telescope: an instrument for looking at distant objects, or for picking up rays that come from them

Universe: all of space and everything in it

volcano: a type of mountain. Volcanoes are formed when very hot, liquid rock is forced up from deep inside a planet. The liquid cools, leaving a mountain of rock

Index